This Journal

Gianna N. Wi

Above all else guard your heart
for it is the wellspring of life.

Proverbs 4:23

Much love, Granna
3/2001